Where must design go next?

with—
Weslynne Ashton
Kim Erwin
Tomoko Ichikawa
Anijo Mathew
Matt Mayfield
John Payne
Zach Pino
Ruth Schmidt
Maura Shea
Carlos Teixeira
Martin Thaler

Edited by—
Jarrett Fuller

**Institute of Design (ID)
at Illinois Tech**

T0044124

ORO
EDITIONS

Novato, CA

Where must design go next?

Edited by—
Jarrett Fuller

ORO Editions
Publishers of Architecture, Art, and Design
Gordon Goff: Publisher

www.oroeditions.com
info@oroeditions.com

Published by ORO Editions

Author: Jarrett Fuller
Book Design: Jarrett Fuller

10 9 8 7 6 5 4 3 2 1 First Edition

ISBN: 978-1-961856-09-7

Prepress and Print work by The Graphic Arts Studio.
Printed in Barrington, IL

ORO Editions makes a continuous effort to minimize the overall
carbon footprint of its publications. As part of this goal, ORO,
in association with Global ReLeaf, arranges to plant trees to
replace those used in the manufacturing of the paper produced
for its books. Global ReLeaf is an international campaign
run by American Forests, one of the world's oldest nonprofit
conservation organizations. Global ReLeaf is American Forests'
education and action program that helps individuals, organizations, agencies, and corporations improve the local and global
environment by planting and caring for trees.

Foreword

Over the last eighty-five years, the Institute of Design (ID) has pioneered three distinct design eras, all of which build on the strengths of previous generations.

The full impact of our fourth and current era is yet to be determined, but you may notice some strong currents and clues to the lessons of this era. All of ID's award-winning work springs from collaborations: ID students, their faculty, and often other partners.

At ID, in our classes and Action Labs, we understand that we cannot and do not solve the complex problems of our time by looking inward, working alone.

Design is a catalyst. We cannot speculate, create, and implement on our own. For too long, designers have lived with the misguided belief that only we can do what we do – the false idea that somehow designers are unique.

In this current phase, ID is powering a new generation of design leaders willing to release the hubris and openly embrace collaboration. They will solve multigenerational problems with the kind of impact that reverberates not just for you and me but for our children, their children, and beyond.

—Anijo Mathew
Dean
Institute of Design (ID)

What is design?

What is design? The joke goes that if you ask 100 designers to define design, you'll receive 100 different answers. Design is both a noun and a verb, a process and a product, an action and a result. It shapes how we live at the micro and macro scales, from the typography on the phones in our pockets to streets we drive on, to the systems that provide services to us on a daily basis. Designers are both problem-solvers and cultural inventors, working with other disciplines to meet the needs of end users and imagine new, more equitable, and sustainable futures.

I had the honor of serving as the 2022-23 Latham Fellow at the Institute of Design (ID) at Illinois Tech. My fellowship, coinciding with the school's eighty-fifth anniversary, provided an opportunity to witness the compelling work and ideas that are energizing the ID community today. Dean Anijo Mathew articulated four eras in the school's history: experimentation, systems, design thinking, and a current, as-yet-unnamed era. These eras, I believe, are not simply the history of ID but also the history of design. Each era doesn't replace the one before it but rather expands upon it, therefore expanding the role and responsibility of design and the mandate of the designer.

For me, this progression raises all sorts of questions, from how we teach the design students of tomorrow, to how designers can find their place in increasingly complex systems, to how we think through our relationship with emerging technology, to how a designer should think about their work beyond the immediate impact. Over the course of my fellowship,

I was fortunate to interview members of the ID faculty to learn their perspectives on the future of design pedagogy and practice. Our wide-ranging conversations, originally recorded for ID's *With Intent* podcast and transcribed in this publication, reflect a driving idea of my work: every generation reinvents design for themselves. I hope that our exchanges point to new – and actionable – definitions that will motivate design education in the years to come.

—Jarrett Fuller
2022–23 Latham Fellow at the Institute of Design

The conversations that follow were recorded, transcribed, and edited slightly to ensure clarity.

Martin Thaler is an associate professor at the Institute of Design (ID), where he focuses on product and environment design.

Tomoko Ichikawa is an associate teaching professor at ID, where she focuses on visual communication.

How does someone become a designer?

–with Tomoko Ichikawa & Martin Thaler

Foundation courses in art and design schools are one of the most enduring legacies of the Bauhaus. Foundation courses focus on materials and processes, and as their name implies, they provide the basis for one's forthcoming design education. When László Moholy-Nagy started The New Bauhaus in Chicago (today's Institute of Design), he brought these courses with him to serve as the core curriculum for all students. I took foundation courses when I studied graphic design fifteen years ago, and many design students – across virtually all design fields – take them today.

But what is the purpose of Foundation at ID? Why has

this model endured? What should Foundation classes look like today to train future designers?

One of the legacies of the Bauhaus was this idea of Foundation courses: this set of classes that every student would take that gives everyone a sense of tools and ideologies and ways of thinking to be a designer. This is something that Moholy-Nagy brought over when he started what is now the Institute of Design.

I found a memo that listed what would be taken in the Foundations courses when the school started. In the first semester, he writes that the emphasis is on tools, technique, and analysis of form and space. The second semester is on technical perfection and further analysis of form. And then the third semester is on presentation and sociological functions. Hearing that, how does that resonate with how you think about Foundation courses today at ID?

TI I share a framework at the beginning of my first week to situate the students in terms of what they're learning over fourteen weeks:

The first five weeks are all about elements and concepts: What are the elements of two-dimensional design? Typography, graphic elements, imagery, etc. What are the techniques and concepts? How do you know when you have contrast? What do you do to attain visual hierarchy?

Then the second five weeks of the class is about applying actual information content matter, so that it is about analyzing the information and figuring out how you use those elements that we just taught you in the first third of the class.

The last capstone project is about understanding the social context. We do a live project using a real scenario that is lacking in terms of good visual design, and we try to get the students to work on that.

So hearing this, I'm thinking "Wow, it's kind of alarming that I'm still using that basic framework!" I don't know if that's good or bad. We have some evolution, yet there are some things that are perennial. I think the Foundation program is a bridge from the

INSTITUTE OF DESIGN

FOUNDATION COURSE (general program)

during the <u>first semester</u> foundation course psychological
rigidity is replaced with stimuli for emotional freedom,
through a basic familiarity with the manipulation
of tools and materials, combined with experimental
analyses in techniques.
this semester's emphasis is on tools, techniques, and a
basic analysis of form and space.

in the <u>second semester</u> foundation course an additional
understanding of new tools, new materials, and new
techniques is combined with a controlled mastery of all
media.
this semester's emphasis is on technical perfection and
a further analysis of form.

during the <u>third semester</u> foundation course technical
knowledge is directly applied to workshop methods and
practice, combining this with an historical and
ideological orientation.
this semester's emphasis is on presentation and
sociological function.

16

non-design world into a design world so that they could be proficient enough to go into the main MDes program.

I think that the perennial nature of these ideas is the key here. You mentioned that your class is focused on communication design or graphic design: typography, contrast, layout, etc. Marty, you come from an industrial design background. What's happening in your Foundation class?

MT My class is also very foundational, and I also see it as a bridge. What's wonderful about it is we get people from all areas. It's one of the few programs at the graduate level that welcomes students from every background. They can enter the school without a design background, which makes for very interesting work. Many people come to the school and have never built anything, made things, or have the know-how needed to actually build prototypes and physical objects. The philosophy of the school is that people need that knowledge because it's a way of thinking as a designer, whether you end up designing objects or communications or strategies or service design. I've always thought that all those principles are interconnected. There is some underlying structure there.

We start with very basic modeling techniques with chipboard. It used to be Foamcore, but I'm a little concerned about the environmental impact. We follow a similar process to Tomoko's class: we try to progress slowly from the early stages of making simple objects to a more complete complex problem that we solve towards the end of the semester. It does take time. It's a field that needs iteration. You can't jump to something very difficult; you have to start with the simple things and then progress. That's a struggle.

TI Foundation is four different classes. Marty teaches Objects and Artifacts and I teach Visual Communication. But there's also photography and interaction design. All the Foundation students need to take all four classes. The idea is that we're

17

trying to make them a more well-rounded design student so that they can enter the MDes program. The students that we get coming straight into the MDes program who have a background in design are often highly specialized – they're either web designers or graphic designers, etc. – and they lack that well-roundedness, which we think is required. Our Foundation students bring in a lot that is not of design too, and that's extremely valuable.

> **Could you speak a little bit to this interdisciplinarity of design? Your students are coming in with either a highly specialized form of design or no design background at all, and they're all going to be mixed together, and they're all going to do different things. How do you think about what students should know as they go through their time at ID?**

TI   I think that what we're asking our students to do is not the end product. Because we are a graduate level school, the things that they think about are much more complex, things that have to do with sustainability or healthcare or civic design. The idea is that we are training our students with these foundational skills so that they can then participate in that larger thinking and communicate broad ideas, either through diagramming or good communication design skills or good prototyping skills. So it's not about perfecting the product design skills, and it's not about perfecting the two-dimensional design skills. It's so that they can then apply them to much bigger things.

MT   What I emphasize in my Object and Artifacts class is understanding the design process itself. It's about an approach, a way to communicate your ideas, creating a way to think about them and present them so that people can work together. So the other thing they get out of Foundations is that there's a real strong sense of community that's built. Foundation students have played a strong role in the culture of the Institute of Design.

18

This makes me think about how so much of design is increasingly intangible — it's about creating services or systems. It's hard to actually look at the thing that has been designed. How do you think about that in the Foundation classes when you're doing modeling, for example, and thinking that a lot of these students might end up designing things that don't actually have a physical form?

MT When you deal with the tangible thing, it's easier to explain values of this detail or the way that it fits into a system. Our last project, for example, is about the future of work. It started years ago, more as "Let's do the next generation of an in-office product that holds your papers under your desk like in the old days." Then, of course, it's become very topical and much more interesting. Now the students get to learn to think about how their object can help people, whether it's going to help them doing their work in a hybrid work environment or a range of other contexts.

TI The idea is that we have to communicate these ideas really well so that people can envision what it's going to be like. That's where the communication design comes into play. It's not graphic design – it's communication design. It's very purposeful and intent-driven. Iterative prototyping is alive and well! How do we get people to iterate where every iteration gets better and better and moves the idea foreward. The ability to communicate your ideas to whomever you are with, even if it's to your own teammates, so that you can get alignment around them, that comes from understanding what it is that you are trying to communicate. It's intent-driven communication rather than form-driven communication.

This speaks to critique, too. Students are very fearful at first, because they often don't come from a critique culture. So even teaching them the right kind of language: that it's not personal, that we don't use "I like" or "I don't like." The bigger goal, then, becomes elevating the work of a team. Big design projects are not possible for one person to

19

Design isn't really for design. Design is for the world.

Design always works with other disciplines.
—Tomoko Ichikawa

solve alone, and there's always going to be other people that they're going to be working with.

So it's not just craft but also about their thinking and approach. Then, maybe, even their own identity changes somewhere during the semester where they can say, "I am a designer now," as opposed to, "I am an electrical engineer." We try to foster those moments where they can recognize that transformation within themselves.

Where, if at all, does software and technology fit in here?

TI Tools are tools, and the idea is that we use tools as a means to accomplish things. Understanding the basic principles of design, such as contrast or visual hierarchy, composition and layout, it doesn't matter if you do that in PageMaker or Quark or InDesign, or even by hand if you wanted to. It's about being able to understand what it is that they are, first and foremost, trying to accomplish, what kind of principles they want to apply, what kind of approaches. The tool just becomes a way to serve that aspiration.

MT One thing that we introduced a long time ago is having a sketchbook, which was just fantastic. We encourage students to use their notebooks to keep track of their ideas or develop ideas and use paper. I think because of the digital nature of what they're doing, it's harder to get them to draw.

TI It is harder because they want to sit in front of the computer first. But if you get them to understand the process, I think they understand that you should actually work out a sketch first. I always tell them that the computer programs actually are prematurely asking them to make decisions about things before they even know. I require my students, along with their finished digital assignments, to provide sketches of their idea development. My co-instructor, Jody Campbell, who I teach the class with, and I are firm believers that this is an important step for them to do first. There have been studies done where the hand, eye, and brain coordination is actually very powerful, and it helps you to think about things that you may not when you're sitting in front of a computer. Physicality is absolutely critical, and I think it's because it's on all the time. It's there in front of you all the time. Whereas if you're working on your computer, you turn it off and you close your laptop and it's gone.

I watched a beautiful commencement speech from one of your former students, Justin Bartkus*, and he had a line in there where he says, "ID doesn't erase our unique set of skills, experiences, and quirks; rather it embraces them, equips them, and amplifies them. We come as engineers, architects, business folks, theologians, and we leave as engineer-designers, architect-designers, business-designers, theologian-designers." He calls this "the dash-designer." Could you talk about how you think about teaching these sets of skills, teaching these ways of working, teaching these processes, while also embracing and encouraging and incorporating this range of experiences that every student is bringing in?

TI If I may, I think they're coming to the Institute of Design to become something bigger, and they're coming to the Institute of Design, like Marty said, not to become product designers or graphic designers. So they're bringing their collective background and during the time of Foundation, it's like we're asking them to squeeze into and hyperfocus, but once they get into the main program, they expand back out again so that they can work in this much larger context of the world. I love Justin's articulation of that, the dash-designer or the design-plus. It goes back to the idea that design isn't really for design. Design is for the world. Design always works with other disciplines.

* Justin Bartkus, "We Have Become Dash-Designers," *Medium* (Institute of Design, May 17, 2021), https://medium.com/iit-institute-of-design/we-have-become-dash-designers-23287b030fcb.

22

Foundation students come and see the other design students doing incredible work, and they often feel bad about that. They think they come from a point of deficiency: "I am not a designer; I don't have the design skills." We try to encourage them to say, "Well, you have all this other skill. It's not a deficiency. It's layers where you are taking what you bring and then layering design on top."

MT From my perspective, I try to emphasize with them. Even if they didn't go to a traditional design program, that they do have a beginner's mind, that can be a real advantage if you use it properly. We've seen it over and over again.

Matt Mayfield is associate dean of academics and administration at ID and director of the Master of Design and Master of Design Methods graduate programs.

Zach Pino is an assistant professor of data-driven design at ID, where he designs with generative algorithms, machine learning models, wearable technologies, and reactive materiality.

How do you teach design for tomorrow?

—with Matt Mayfield & Zach Pino

The design fields are in the midst of rapid change – technological, cultural, political, and societal. Designers consistently find themselves in new domains and working with new tools. The old frameworks for design education – which presume certain processes, tools, and outcomes – are no longer sufficient.

How do you teach students design today for an uncertain future? What does it mean to teach design today? What do today's design students need to know to practice design? What is the value of design education and its role in the industry?

Matt, you're the associate dean of academics and administration and oversee all the curriculum at ID. How do you think about the curriculum? Can you talk about the process of putting a curriculum together in an institution like ID?

MM   One of the things that's important to say is we didn't start from scratch. We came into a school that was very established, doing very well, and had found its way through the changes in design over the years. So part of the challenge was how do we continue that progress? How do we continue its strength while also being open to changes? In moving into this role, one of the things that I really wanted to stay focused on was preserving that flexibility and that ability to continually refresh without having to rethink the entire thing.

That's where I think curriculum and schools can sometimes get in trouble. They're like, "OK, we feel a little out of step, let's rethink the whole thing." Then it takes two years and lots of debate, yet students are going through and they're learning. I'm happy that we've got such a gracious faculty that's willing to go along with the idea that we do have to adjust and integrate new ideas as they come in.

On the other side, we think about the student journey and where they're coming from. As a graduate-only school, we have a luxury – which we protect a lot – that most of these students have professional experience. They've had some time to mature so we're not going to worry as much about basics, about whether design is something that they should consider as a focus in their education, or whether they think they can build a career out of it. They've worked through that already and we can come in and say, "Yes, we all agree. Design is a really interesting field. There's lots to learn here and lots to use. Now let's take that step."

I have been lucky to start with those very strong points of flexibility and a fairly well-developed student body so that we can step into some bigger issues. We still have challenges, of course. Like anybody else, it's hard to change, but that's where we're starting from.

Can you talk a little bit more about the connections between the history and the present day? What are ideas from the school's history that you think are still important and relevant in the curriculum today? Then, where are you innovating? Where are you trying new things that wouldn't have been there ten or twenty years ago?

MM Some of the throughlines in the curriculum have been the importance of experimentation. This goes all the way back to the Bauhaus idea of the capabilities of technology and industry and how, as designers, we can take advantage of these capabilities to build the things we want to build, or at least articulate the futures we see that are more desirable than where we are now. That's always been there, and I think that continues.

Back in the early days, it was much more about physical production and how to make things more reliable and more ergonomic and things like that. I remember as a student, we would be looking at production methods and ways to incorporate all sorts of different really exotic materials like plastic and rubber and all that stuff. We're asking similar questions now, but we're talking about digital capabilities of managing massive amounts of data and interpreting that for an individual specific context.

I think the other part is that we broke free from a strong arts background a while ago. It's never been super strong in our program because we've been more pragmatic – we're more functional in our approach to design for better and for worse. It served us well when we moved into things like design thinking and our relationship with business where we could say design can help make whatever those products and services are better. We still have to define what better is, but that's what designers are really good at. What I'm getting to is that we weren't

27

beholden to notions of artistic expression and that helped us to define other ways of contributing and authoring our work.

> **Zach, you have a background in computer science. You're teaching a lot of digital tools and emerging technologies. I've seen this happen two ways. First, where designers learn about new technologies purely conceptually, basically that these things exist and you should know about, say, artificial intelligence for example. And then on the other side, it's approached really technically where it's like, you need to learn how to use this software or you need to code in this language. But it seems like there must be some sort of balance between those two. How do you approach that? How do you think about introducing new technologies into a curriculum?**

ZP That's a fantastic question. I think fundamentally when I came into ID seven years ago, I came into a school that, as Matt described, was, from my naive point of view, tied much more to the business side than the personal expression side. So a lot of students at that time saw their future as a designer tied to opportunities in consulting, opportunities in entrepreneurship, opportunities in joining in-house design teams that were fairly well-established, but over the last seven years at ID, we've seen this kind of seismic shift in what our students' goals are as designers.

So when I joined ID, students were very interested in picking up very hard technical skills because they knew that in some ways they would be going into the world to deploy design, whether that meant entrepreneurially building a digital product or needing to know enough about technology to communicate with an engineering team within their organization. So in those early years, Matt was really open and flexible to us introducing courses in Python and JavaScript, those kind of very hard technical skills.

In more recent years, however, we've seen students with much, much less – almost zero – interest in that kind of engagement with technology, which we suspect is very much tied to changing social dynamics, relationships with technology, and presumptions and perceptions of technology. Instead we see our students wanting to be working at a higher level and engaging engineering processes and engineering teams with critical oversight. Our curriculum has needed to shift to accommodate that new goal that our students might have in their professional careers after graduate school, which means we are teaching not, "This is how to write this kind of function in Python" – though we certainly still do that – but now we also have courses like surveys in emergent technology, studio courses in data visualization, where we're not teaching students how to necessarily write all of the code for making interactive data visualizations, but exposing students to data visualization tools and disciplinary norms, then allowing them to explore what would it mean to hand draw a data visualization. As Matt hinted at, returning almost to the personal expression and personal agency associated with a traditional art and design program.

I think one of the challenges in design education today — and this comes up in so many conversations that I have with educators — is that the field of design is so big. The areas into which students can go in is infinite. You could go into data visualization, you could go into systems design, you could go into interface design. So there's this tension between surveying all the opportunities and presenting the range of work while also having to go deep on some of those because it can't just be this cursory look.

How much of this is student-driven? Are students sort of coming into the class saying, "We're interested in these things," and then you're tailoring these surveys to that, as opposed to saying, "Here are some things that I think are interesting, here are some emerging practices, emerging technologies, and I'm going to show these to you?"

ZP   I'm confident that in our courses, the model student needs exposure to contemporary technologies more than they need any degree of mastery over those technologies. Trends in technological development today have facilitated that new orientation for our student body. We've seen this incredible convergence from where we were several years ago, which, as you described, was a very wide and diverse, but disparate, set of technical competencies where data visualization is going to be different than interaction design, which is going to be different from CAD, 3D modeling for fabrication.

In the last several years, certainly in the COVID and post-COVID time, there's been this massive alignment and convergence in data-oriented practice, where every discipline of design and every technical vertical that a student might be interested in pursuing is going to be centered deeply in engagement with data and engagement with computational intelligence and computational creativity. And because of that alignment, it becomes a lot easier for us to teach that. Because we can go deep into what data is – these are the dimensions of data quality, these are the metrics by which we would evaluate to what degree a data set is valuable in design insight making – we don't need to necessarily cover the waterfront.

MM   I believe designers can be more inspired when they have a little bit more than just awareness of something. They have to play with it. They have to say, "Oh, wait, this can do this. What if I do this?" That's where we get that fun creativity.

For me, I want to get our students to the point where they can play with technology. We're not going to ever say, "OK, you are a certified engineer putting out commercial grade solutions," but we do want them to be able to engage engineers, or whoever is involved with the development at these different levels, at a higher level: Are we doing this ethically? Are we being equitable? Where are our blind spots with how we are using this technology or the ways we see it progressing? But also at a lower level where it's also, "Hey, did we ever think about trying this? Would that be valuable?"

That's the key question for all of our students: Where is the value? I'm purposefully making that a very ambiguous term because that's the discussion. What do we mean by value? Where is it? How can we get to it? Does everyone agree on that value? So being able to poke around in the technology enough to get a feel for it to understand the power, because a lot of it is abstract when you say, "Machine learning takes in troves and troves of information." Do you really know what that means? You could say it, but do you really feel it? That middle ground in exploring is where I get most excited. So we do try to respond to students where they're at and where they're going, but also to challenge. Why are we learning this? Where is this going to help us in our practice as designers?

> **Speaking of value, I want to turn that back on the education experience. I think graduate design education is in an interesting spot where it can also do all sorts of things. There is some sense of job preparation, of understanding the field and giving you skills to go work in the field. There's some sense of experimentation, that grad school is a laboratory to try things, to be critical, to be provocative, to challenge things. There's some sense of graduate school being a chance to redefine the field, to redefine design, to challenge industry, to push industry forward. It's a little of all of those plus more. How do you think about the role of graduate design education? What is the value that students get out of those two years?**

MM It's a great question. For our school, and the students that we attract and the students that are successful coming through our program, they're not coming to us saying, "I want to get a job in UX, and I'm going to come here to get trained to do that." We think that's a bit of a flag because yes, it's possible to do that, but that's really not what the full experience can be. That full experience is a time to reflect. That's why we're so excited when we have somebody that has been practicing design for a little while and saying, "Hey, you know what? I think I want to learn more about my field and my practice. I want to explore a little bit, broaden my horizons." We love that. I think those students do the best in our program, and it's that reflective nature.

For me, that's where the value is. If we want to get it down to the crass exchange here, depending on the program, they are choosing to spend a couple of years to step back from their practice, to not be stuck in the constraints of a job-oriented workload, and to give themselves a little bit of freedom to explore and think.

For some students, they just stumbled into their design practice. They learned on their own. They never really had a chance to examine it in a more formal setting. So we can support that – not just with the faculty, but with other students. I think that's where our program is strongest: within the cohort, the community of students that are able to bring different perspectives, and different experiences.

These students want to be masters in design. How do we get them to be masters? What does that mean? The ability to have a lot of perspectives and be able to ask great, important questions that open up conversations, that move things forward, that bring insight to the debate, that are able to inspire others to see maybe the opportunities in a different way.

To me, if a student walks out of here doing that, they've gotten what they came for. They are well-positioned to influence wherever they land, and whoever they work with because they won't be doing it alone. That's where I kind of anchor the value of at least our program.

ZP What's so hard about any sort of engagement with a graduate curriculum is that you are, in the case of many of our students, coming into a new discipline or some kind of minor to extreme reorientation within your discipline. Everyone in a graduate program is going to be talking almost exclusively about how quickly the field is changing. And that is especially true of design.

Design was very well-defined and established in the '90s and early aughts. Ever since, it has really been challenged in almost every flank, whether that's the implications of being a creator in a world with significant sustainability challenges or being a responsible researcher, but also being tied to certain kinds of ill-defined business metrics and timelines.

So our students are coming in and they're seeking clarity. They're seeking a lane to place themselves in, and all we can do is tell them there are no lanes right now, or the lanes are yet to be established. The students who are most effective here at ID, from my point of view, are those that are willing to embrace that ambiguity and recognize that their time with us is to help establish those lanes for the next generation of designers and design students.

MM   I do think that's where design is most exciting. It is in the new intersections, in the new applications, in the new types of jobs. When I graduated from my undergraduate in design, we essentially focused on design thinking, but no one recognized it that way. No companies were hiring design thinkers. It wasn't there. But there was the confidence that I could add value; it just took time to figure out how to define that in the terms of the day. It is challenging in that it's a field in flux, but the most exciting part is that flux gives you opportunity.

> I want to go back to an idea that's come up again and again about this push and pull of artistic expression. So much early design theory and history was really about separating design from art. Certainly, on the surface level, those can feel at odds with each other: you have human-centered methodologies, developing personas and user

You are not a machine to make objective work.

Design is still very much, I believe, a subjective field.

It's an interpretation of what we think should be or could be or ought to be.
—Matt Mayfield

experience, and all of these things on one side, and then the designer's point of view, of expression, of authorship on the other. How do you blend these? How do you show that both of these things can happen at the same time?

MM   Most of the classes I teach are business-oriented: how to plan product lines and how to think about what's next with more sophisticated products. That being said, I talk a lot about how the work we do in design – and thinking about what's possible – has to be grounded in research and information. We want to make good decisions. There is a point in every project, in everything that you do as a designer, where you are interpreting. You have an authorship role in how this work is being handled, how you adjust, and how you conform to your constraints. That's you making choices, and I think we should embrace that.

It may not be the free form expression of art, but there is an authorship. There is a decision to say, "This is the way I'm looking at this problem. This is the way that I chose to shape it, interpret what we're seeing with a team or without a team." You should embrace that. You do have a place in this. You do have a voice. We obviously have biases and we have all sorts of blind spots, so you have to be aware of that. So pay attention to it, but don't ever suppress your voice. You are not a machine to make objective work. Design is still very much, I believe, a subjective field. It's an interpretation of what we think should be or could be or ought to be. Those are the things that designers should be thinking about, and you can't remove yourself from that conversation.

ZP   I, like many of our students, entered design not from a straight path. The field that I entered circa mid-2010s was really a field that had over-expressed and overexerted itself so much into adjacent disciplines, whether that was the social sciences or engineering, that it had, in some ways, lost a sense of itself and its own core value and competencies.

So this kind of retreat that many of the design disciplines have gone through in the last ten years or so really reflects this recognition that design had not only overexerted itself, but it had become reliant on a very kind of convoluted self justification: "I'm going to go out into the world and I'm going to say this is what the world is asking for. That's the problem. I'm calling that the problem and now I'm going to solve it, and here's my answer to that problem." It creates this weird circular logic that's still deeply embedded in a lot of traditional design practice and business-oriented design practices where you lose sight of the fact that you are a creator. You are identifying this particular set of issues to address with your creative outputs.

That, for many of our students, is incredibly refreshing because they're wanting to bring this value-driven or ethics-driven motivation. They're working on behalf of inclusion, equity, and sustainability. They're wanting the work to reflect their vision and not mask that in what the company is asking of them in the brief, or some set of personas that they've developed and artificial problems they've identified.

What about design is exciting you right now?

MM There's an optimism that's coming in. Designers can't stop at outrage or critical thinking. We have to say, "What do we do about that? Where do we go?" I feel very encouraged that these students are going to go out and make fantastic impacts in the world because they can bring that optimism and those values into their work.

ZP I am extraordinarily driven at this particular moment in design by the fact that today's design does not need to be resolved fully or even fully understood by the designer when it is introduced into the world. I know that that sounds really scary and that I might be promulgating a certain kind of sloppiness with design practice, but with so many data-oriented tools and computationally intelligent tools today, we have this remarkable capability to design and experience 80 percent, 50 percent, 20 percent, and then let context and dynamics and preferences and dimensions of the human engaging our designs fill in that remaining space. As I say, that is often scary at the moment, and we're seeing the limitations and weaknesses and over-exuberance by many computational designers, but this opportunity to create not singular, fully understood designs, but rather incredibly intricate, complicated, flexible, dynamic multiples of our experience, that as a designer I might not ever fully comprehend, is really just a tremendous moment in design.

Ruth Schmidt is an associate professor at ID, where she focuses on behavioral design.

Carlos Teixeira is the Charles L. Owen Professor of Systems Design at ID, where he teaches graduate courses. He also advises doctoral students on the strategic use of design capabilities in complex spaces of innovation.

What if human-centered design isn't enough?

—with Ruth Schmidt & Carlos Teixeira

In the last two decades, nearly every design field has been transformed by the development of human-centered design. Where design decisions were previously driven by a designer's preferences, manufacturing capabilities, or market competition, human-centered design shifted the focus of design from the object itself to the context of the end user. This change led to a revolution in design processes, but somewhere along the way human-centered design started to lose its way.

Is human-centered design really the goal we should be focused on? Does it overlook non-human design, for example, or ignore environmental issues? How can we think about design that is, perhaps, ecology-centered, or as ID faculty Ruth Schmidt refers to it: "humanity-centered design"?

What is "humanity-centered design" and how is it different than the more common term "human-centered design?"

RS I got a master's here at ID, and human-centered design was the name of the game. That really was where the action was at the time, but more recently – partly because of where human-centered design as a whole is going and partly because of where my natural interests and research were leading – it's been demonstrated in a variety of settings that only designing for humans can actually lead us down a dangerous path. We satisfy human needs at the expense of non-human elements like the planet; we're not thinking about systemic effects.

For example, you could argue that human-centered design has actually led to a bunch of dangerous habits when it comes to using digital devices. We can lean into human tendencies by having them use infinite scroll, but we all know that that's actually not such a great thing for people to do.

So humanity-centered design is a step to the right place where we want to go. It's an effort to connect what has normally been centered on people but accept that humanity is a much bigger set of concerns because it's about the sustainability of our planet or how we interact and work in systems.

Ruth, your work is about this relationship between behavioral science and design. How do those two fields come together? What does that actually look like in your work?

RS Behavioral design is a fairly new field. The field itself started in the '70s, and it's a more scientific way of understanding people's behavior. It's looking at all the ways in which we're "irrational," for example why we grab the cookie instead of the apple even though we know we shouldn't. We're terrible about planning for the future, even though we know better. Behavioral design tries to understand all of these tendencies that we have that are not necessarily in our best interest. That field hit the mainstream in about 2008, which is when I was here getting my master's.

I was already steeped in human-centered design, and as I started to become aware of this other field, found them to be a beautiful complement. It's a way of understanding different aspects of how people act, make decisions, and make judgments. After spending time using those insights in professional practice, I now focus on how to make designers conversant and comfortable with behavioral science so they can bring that into their practice. And on the flip side, I talk to behavioral scientists and help them understand the importance and the value of design because if you're only designing for behavior, you're actually leaving a bunch of really, really important stuff out.

Carlos, in your biography, it says that your research is centered around the question, "How can design affect the lives and wellbeing of people and communities by leveraging the interconnectivity of markets, technology, environment, finance, and social networks?" So I'm going to ask you that. How can design affect the lives and well-being of people and communities by leveraging the interconnectivity of markets, technology, environments, finance, and social networks? What does that research look like right now?

CT   To put the question in context, it's based on trying to move the understanding of products and services beyond focusing on the product in itself and designing the products for industrial production. You have the human-centered design approach – understanding those products as they interact with humans in their daily lives and their experiences – but what we are saying is that those products, in reality, happen at the intersection of multiple systems. I like to think about projects and services as things in a larger context.

For example, if you just think about bike sharing, we can think about a service for micro-mobility. But in reality, it is something that has multiple intersections: it relates to payments that you do; it relates to exercise that you use the bike; it relates to mobility; it relates to commerce depending on where you're putting those bike stations and the local commerce that you are enabling around that. So when you start to look at those products and services in the larger context in which they exist – not only as it relates to the user experience – then you're going to see that there are multiple intersections happening all the time.

A lot of what we call human-centered design is really a corporation-centered design. I think when we think about design in these systems and in these contexts, often what we are centering is profit, attention, eyeballs, etc. What do you think about this trajectory of human-centered design and its relationship to, in most cases, profit and business use cases?

RS   It's a really wonderful question in part because there are probably many causes. It's interesting, because I think this is part of the DNA of ID under the leadership of Jay Doblin, the idea that you could combine business and design and strategy was at the time really new and exciting and novel. That instinct, which is interesting and powerful, is still there but it has also taken on a life of its own.

I was one of these people who went into consulting, for example. People need to get jobs after graduating and what happens is you end up working in the service of somebody who is there to make a profit. So human-centered design is not evil or good, but it certainly is taking the skillset of what designers are good at and sending it in a direction where there is a lot of capitalist momentum behind it. Getting eyeballs on things and selling things that people want to purchase has gotten very, very intertwined, I think, with where human-centered design has led us. It's not exclusive to that, but it has definitely been a contributing factor.

CT   One of the key novelties of human-centered design was the idea that when we are designing, we need to shift our focus from looking at the product itself to considering the context of daily activities. Human-centered design was not a commercial issue or a corporate issue. It was about how to understand the products as they exist and the agency they have in the daily life. Products in the past were designed as the result of industrial production but also as part of market competition. Everything was about market share, where and how do we beat the competition. This does not necessarily always create the best product for the consumer; it's just creating something that competes better in the marketplace. Human-centered design, then, was picked up by corporations as a business strategy where you'd find products that fit better in people's daily lives and entire markets could be created around that.

How do we get back to this idea of focusing on activities, responding to the needs of people, as opposed to market share? It seems like some of that has gotten lost in the discourse. How are you making sure that stays a focus in the classroom?

CT   We need to see that there are unintended consequences of focusing on the user experience. For example, when we design for the user, we often focus on convenience, but making everything very convenient for the user can generate a lot of waste.

Think about the bike sharing example again: people having the convenience of paying with a credit card. This is fantastic. But this is also discriminatory, because people that don't have credit and financial access are discriminated against using bike sharing. In focusing on convenience again, it becomes something that is for the privileged, the ones that can be consumers, those that can afford the better quality products.

This connects to this shift from human-centered, which sounds like a single person, to humanity-centered, where it is about all of us collectively. What does that mean when we're thinking about us as a species as opposed to us as a human?

Being a good
designer means
being a good
critical thinker.

It's about looking
at all of these
questions and
interrogating the
choices you're
making and having
different lenses
to understand the
implications of
choices.

—Ruth Schmidt

I'm wondering if that can even be pushed further: What does a eco-centered design look like, for example, or an environment-centered design?

RS   I would argue that questions about what progress looks like are really important to consider here because we tend to think of it as questions like: How do I do it faster? How do I get more, cheaper? All of these things that feel beneficial to that end consumer are possibly at the expense of larger systems.

I think reflection is an incredibly important part of design, both as a designer but also just as a person, as a human. We don't often get the chance to reflect when things are happening in a speedy way. Not to pick on Amazon, but anyone who has one-click Amazon setup, as soon as you click it, it's purchased. There's no friction to that process. That can be both for sustainability reasons and waste reasons, but it can also mean that we don't always temper our own behavior.

This question about who has access is incredibly important. Things like the switch from cash to credit cards, which has been coming up in a variety of ways over the past couple of years, is a great example of that. It can seem like we're leaning into progress: you wave a phone, you can buy it. But it leaves whole swaths of populations out, and it means that the difference between who the haves and the have-nots are becomes enormous. I sometimes talk about this notion of choice infrastructure, which is not targeted behavior change, but the whole set of conditions that surround how we make decisions or what we have access to. That sense of humanity is not just about what's good for me or people like me, but recognizing the inequity that gets built into those systems altogether. If human-centered design is not focusing on those things, it's not doing a great job of making sure that we as a society are actually standing up for what we should.

There's a line from the systems theorist Stafford Beer: "The purpose of a system is what it does."

At face value, that seems obvious, but it raises all these questions about unintended consequences. The purpose of a system is not what we say it does, or what it is supposed to do, or what we set out to do, but actually what it does when it is in the world doing what it does. Is this actually what it was designed to do? How do you encourage that kind of thinking in the classroom and with your students?

RS I think being a good designer means being a good critical thinker. When I look back to my own classes, whether it was in college or graduate school, I realize that the things that make me a strong designer are less about specific skills. The things that I find important are about really looking at all of these questions and interrogating the choices you're making and having different lenses to understand the implications of choices.

Even the term "unintended consequences," you could argue about. Maybe they were unintended but sometimes we could've seen that that was going to happen. I find in my behavioral design classes, in particular, a lot of what we work through is how to understand what it is that we're designing into but also how to understand, for example, where there are uncertainties and how to design for uncertainty. What are the conditions? What are the infrastructures? How is that going to support things that we didn't intend but are likely to happen because we're functioning in spaces that encourage certain kinds of behavior over others?

Is part of the responsibility of the designer to make space for that reflection when they are working in these complex systems? There seems to be something about the position of the designer, who can have that overall view of how these systems are coming together, that makes for an interesting place to start to raise these questions.

CT We engage in very deep and extended conversation about this with our students because the tendency, when we look at those systems, is for us to try to be the superhero. Design is the one that can understand the whole, can understand all the specifics, can be fully interdisciplinary, transdisciplinary, cross-disciplinary, and be at the center and do everything and solve all the problems. I think this is one very dangerous and very problematic extreme. For me, designers have a unique position, which is the expertise on products and services. We have a long history of that, and I think we need to be able to leverage that expertise as it relates to systems.

I see a lot of other fields that can deal with systems much better than designers. Policy makers, engineers, and many others, for example, can think about the totality of systems. They can think about the parts and their connections. What I think is exclusive to designers is that most of the people that are thinking about systems, they are thinking at the macro level and the meso level, but they're not thinking at the micro level, where products and services exist. They can never explain how something like the like button has a major impact on how people are categorized in different groups, how they create echo chambers of discussions, etc. As we are entering this new era of design, I strongly believe that designers need to leverage the expertise on product, services, and communication, but they need to contextualize that in larger systems and work with the other disciplines to show the role that those things play in the larger context.

Can design help businesses think beyond short-term profit or think through these ideas about climate change, about inequalities, about democracy? How can design help others think about systems at these micro and macro levels?

RS Similarly to how Carlos was just describing the macro, meso, micro in terms of systems, we can think about that happening within commercial organizations. There are decisions that are happening at that high strategic level, there's the middle level of deciding how to execute on things or how they're organized to do that, and then there's the lowest level of actually doing those things and getting products out the door, making decisions around how to build an app or how to deliver services. Part of what I think makes it complicated is that when we train our students here, they go into practice and they don't jump right to the top of the food chain.

Plus, there's not one kind of design. How people think about design's value has always been a little tricky because it's not always easily measurable. And so whether that's value towards really positive, beneficial ends that are more broad in society or how we think about design use to create individual services or offerings.

We're having so many more conversations at school about these issues than we certainly did when I was here as a student. When I was here about thirteen years ago as a student, we just didn't talk as much about power or equity or how design can contribute in different ways. There's been a real change I think just in terms of like, "Hey, this is something that we can't control only by ourselves." But we better talk about it because we can't be sending people out into the world who are not considering the implications of what they bring.

CT I strongly believe that the way that we're going to deal with those large systems – what I call complex spaces of innovation, because they are at the intersection of multiple systems – is that we're going to depend on large corporations or large organizations because they are the ones that have the resources; they are the ones that have the talent; they are the ones that can do long-term investment; they have the expertise to do imple-mentation, and they can stand resiliently through a process of transformation. It can be government agencies, universities, corporations, foundations, and we have to think about where design is situated in them and how we can have the greatest impact by situating design strategically where these deci-sions are taking place. Design is the field that's going to bring choices rather than just decisions to those organizations. So I think we need to deconstruct a lot of the current design practices and start to imagine new design practices in new kinds of organizations.

Kim Erwin is an associate
professor at ID, where
she focuses on healthcare
design and design methods.

Maura Shea is an associate
professor at ID, where
she focuses on evolving
community-led development
methods and approaches.

Why is design always talking about complexity?

–with Kim Erwin & Maura Shea

One of the biggest shifts in the history of design is the move from object to system. Historically, design could feel superficial – something that happened at the end of a process to help a product or service go to market. No longer relegated to mere decorating, design is integral to the entire process. No longer is it merely designing a product but also designing the systems that surround it. Design, and designers, are involved in increasingly complex systems to help think about the development of products, processes, organizations, and cultures. In many ways, the role of the designer is more intangible than ever, yet it is also more important.

What does it mean to be a designer when the thing you are designing isn't always a clear, physical object? How does a designer find their place – and their purpose – within a system where the asks are not always clear? How does the role of the designer change when design's role moves from the object to the system?

Maura, you've done a lot of work on thinking about belonging and community and collaboration. Can you talk about your work and research and the types of classes that you're teaching?

MS I came across a guidebook that was published in the early '90s, when I was in the YMCA's archives that resonated with me because I recognized in my work in national nonprofit networks how the position of design needs to be informed by the assets that exist in any community. I'm really interested in being influenced by other fields and other ways of thinking about the human experience beyond what human-centered design has offered me.

I'm currently teaching some core research courses, but I'm also teaching a course that focuses on how we can actually scrutinize the design process and the role of the designer from an approach that came out of the School of Social Policy at Northwestern University and is currently at the DePaul University Steans Center that centers on asset-based community development. Asset-based community development is a way to recognize the assets that already exist in a community, rather than looking at a community around a problem. That's very deficit-minded. So to instead be asset-minded helps us to actually say, "What are the conditions for change? Where are those voices within a community that actually can drive, direct, and ideally, sustain, whatever changes they want to make? How can design build a context, build support for, and enable, in whatever way is appropriate, the kind of conditions for social impact and social change?"

Kim, you've done a lot of work around healthcare design. Can you talk about that work in the classes that you're teaching?

KE I stumbled into healthcare in 2013 when I was invited to participate in a randomized clinical trial to help develop the core intervention in that trial, which turned out to be a piece of communication that is supposed to be delivered by doctors to patients in the emergency department, especially to the pediatric patient population. I really didn't know why I was involved. When I went to the first meeting, they passed the intervention around and I took one look at it and thought, "OK, I know what I could do here." It was something that had a lot of technical and thoughtful information from somebody who thinks about things in a medical sense but wasn't remotely usable from not just an information design perspective but also just from a cultural perspective. How do you give this to parents, especially in the low-income communities that they were supposed to be targeting? That was my introduction and it snowballed from there.

I've been incorporating that into coursework at the Institute of Design in various ways. I just finished teaching my first Healthcare Design class where the focus is introducing students to the complex, invisible, living web of systems that hold current practices in place. Pretty much anyone can walk into a health system and go, "We could do better than this," but there's a reason that it's the way it is and it's not for the lack of knowledge. No one more than healthcare providers understand how poorly structured the care delivery system is in the United States. It's not willful. It's not intentional. That particular course is about how to apprehend the multisystem that is healthcare and figuring out design's role in impacting that. Designers don't – and shouldn't – own the agenda in healthcare. But you need background knowledge. You need domain knowledge. That is what I attempt to do.

I also run healthcare workshops, which bring in sponsored projects and the real world constraints for design. As I like to tell my students, "The problem in healthcare is not the lack of ideas. It's getting anything to happen at all."

For so long and for so many different types of design, the cliche that we always hear is that "design is problem-solving." When you think about design that way, that leads to particular types of practices and particular types of processes. What changes

when we shift from being problem-solvers to asset identifiers? How does that change the role of the designer or the way the designer works within these systems?

MS It's not that problems don't exist. It's not some overly optimistic stance. It's starting from a position of acknowledging and taking inventory of the assets that exist. When you're working within social systems – communities or health systems or even university systems – they have social dynamics that are complex. By visualizing those assets across multilayered systems, we can begin to perceive the context we're working in in new ways. That inherently will affect the ways we define what opportunities there are for design, who should be involved, what kind of objectives and outcomes we're after, and how we would possibly measure any results that we're pursuing.

When I was at IDEO, we would say, "Design is about keeping your head in the clouds and your feet on the ground," which is cute. But what we're trying to do is make positive systemic societal change so we have to be reality-focused. We have to know who is owning any intervention, any solution, any shift of the context, or the conditions for the system to function within. Often that's not the designer.

Kim mentioned earlier that designers can't solve healthcare because designers aren't qualified. So designers have to ask, "Well, what is our role? What do we bring to these complex systems? What are the ways we can identify our set of skills and match those to the issues at hand?" How do you work with students to give them the tools to be able to enter into a diverse, complex, complicated community and find their place or where design is helpful? Which is to say, in finding where design is helpful, it's also identifying where design is not helpful and not needed sometimes.

MS A lot of it is about helping to build capacities to see what alternatives are available where you're role modeling alternative ways of doing

things. For example, I'm co-leading a Food Systems
Action Lab with Professor Weslynne Ashton, and what
we're trying to do there is help facilitate how food
waste is prevented, upcycled, or directed in the
right direction. That's workflow process. Just like
Kim said about the health system, those workflows
are designed in very specific ways over many, many
years, and often for good reason. Designers gener-
ally have to get acquainted with those workflows.
A workflow is a way of connecting nodes. It's about
understanding actors in a system, and how the interactions between those actors exist. It's taking an
inventory of how are those things interacting. Then
we can understand where those shifts in the system
might work differently. That's an imagineering role.
That is very hard for the folks who are doing the
day-to-day work. They're very committed to keeping
the trains running on time, so to shift operations
like this takes some courage, and not everybody has
that creative courage.

> **Kim, in healthcare specifically, how do you think
> about how designers find their place in a system
> like that that is cultural, political, professional?**

KE I focus on this idea of the multisystem. Jay
Doblin in 1987, before he passed away, left us with
one last brilliant piece of writing that he called, in
true Jay Doblin terms, "A Short, Grandiose Theory of
Design." He wrote that designers have to understand
that there are at least three levels of complexity."
Products is the first level. At the product level,
there's a finite number of features and performance
features that somebody needs to manage and these
sorts of things.

Next is systems. Systems-level design puts a product
into a context and says, "There's many more forces
at work that this product has to be situated in." If
you're designing an airline seat, for example, you
have to start thinking about how people order food,
where they put their baggage, or how the seat fits
into the temporary communal aspect of flying.

Doblin, then, saw a third level coming, which was very prescient. The third one he called "the multisystem." The multisystem is a system of systems, and he compared it to not just an airline seat in an airplane, but in an airline system where there is baggage check and TSA and retail and scheduling systems.

That's a different role for a designer. So when I work with my students, I talk about the multisystem and I say, "Healthcare's too big to know." It just is. It's ginormous. So you need new tools, questions, frameworks, checklists, to help you manage the sheer volume of factors that are going to affect your thinking. To me, it's a mindset of thinking about things as a multisystem and knowing that your design has to be systems-aware.

This is one of the big shifts in design of the last decade or so: design has moved away from objects to systems and increasingly, the thing the designer produces is immaterial. It is the system, it is the visualization. I think that's complicated design's role because before you could say, "Oh, well, we're designing the chair." That's what the designer does. Or, "We're designing the logo, the building, or whatever." But now it is imagining new ways of doing things, it's imagining systems, it's suggesting alternatives. Tell me more about how that changes the role of the designer?

KE I think that one of the challenges is that the designer's role has to shift from just being about the problem-solving and the solution, to being about the human beings and the organization involved in launching that solution. Not people in abstraction or people as users but as your implementers.

MS Hearing your question reminded me of when I would work side-by-side with mechanical engineers. Design was about making not only one prototype, but multiple types of prototypes: works like prototypes, appearance prototypes, and material prototypes. Then with digital, with the experience economy, as manufacturing was moving away from the United States and the digital economy was on the rise, and we were focused more on upfront planning and on product portfolios and the variability that digital design has offered a whole generation of designers. What's the next context that design is trying to function in? I appreciate Kim saying it's relational because that's absolutely right. We are decolonizing design and reckoning with the privileged positions that design has always claimed.

My theory about visualizing them is that it gives us a way to try and make tangible and shareable, and hopefully thus democratic, the systems we're working within. The democratic component is that it's a collective meaning-making. It's not up to the designer to interpret and conclude and summarize and present; it's rather this much more facilitative, interactive interpretation that is led by the folks who will be impacted most by the solutions they devise.

I like this idea of collective meaning-making. What this makes me think about is how this completely flips the script of what we should and could be teaching designers and teaching the next generation of designers. What are the new additions in a design curriculum that are needed? And what are the things from the past that are still important?

MS I'm a graduate of the Institute of Design from the previous millennia, and I graduated with a master's in design as one of the last photographers. I was using photography as a social design research tool, and I was presenting my graduate thesis at the Conference of Visual Sociology. One of my students recently was talking about AI-generated imagery and was able to, within seconds of course, just construct an image that reflected the keywords that he input. It's a totally different process and a different experience, but I was really fascinated by what the artifact itself was able to provide our discussion. How are images used as a communication tool both in generative discussion and in summative discussion? That left me numb for a little bit, because I'm going to stand by craft and production and making as a core skill of design, but are the tools now shifting that relationship so tremendously that I don't even recognize that process?

KE I think the skillset that we should keep teaching, but maybe teach it more expansively, is this reliance on user research. User research has ethnographic roots – most ethnographers would cringe at the fortune of their practices in design – but ethnographic perspective says you're going to look at functional aspects of an activity system. So if I'm going into an emergency department, I'm going to look at all the users and all their activities and all their interactions and objects. It also says that we would look at that as a human system. It's also a workplace, and as a workplace, it has culture. As a culture, it has relationships.

When we think of user observation and other ex-ploratory mechanisms that we call user research, we should also be teaching people how to turn that on your organization that you're working with so they can be equally open and curious and understand the human interactions in the organization. They will help you be a better designer. They will help you understand who needs to see what. All of those skill sets transfer, but we don't teach them that way. We are always focused on end users, without thinking about the organization as being a stakeholder that we should be considering.

I don't think it's about the visualization; I think it's about the visualizing. It's not the user re-search, it's the researching. It's not the prototype, it's the prototyping. That's all still relevant.

I think it's interesting that we can talk about these tools, these processes, as not just for designers anymore. Are these actually principles that are more widely helpful? Do we even need to think of them as design, or can these ideas actually be expanded, so different types of people and differ-ent types of industries who would never use the word design can actually apply them in their work,

61

I don't think it's about the visualization.
I think it's about the visualizing.

It's not the user research; it's the researching.

It's not the prototype; it's the prototyping.
—Kim Erwin

in their communities, in their organizations, in their systems?

MS I left ID and spent almost a decade at IDEO where innovation was really the work. We were talking about it from a human-centered design methodology, but I was able to encounter all kinds of innovators who came from different fields, from creative problem-solving to group facilitation experts to business perspectives and so forth.

Design is just one approach to addressing the challenges that we're talking about and to engaging across sectors to solve some of these problems. I don't know that design has a monopoly on anything, but it does have some skill sets that can be brought in to be contributive.

KE Herbert Simon defined design as the mechanism that takes something from a current state to a preferred state. That's designing, not necessarily designers. What we saw in the '90s was this proliferation of the term "design thinking" and a dissemination of basic design strategy into the population. People have different points of view on that, but I think it's nice that people actually know that that's a term now, so it's definitely broadened the target market.

So do I think design has a distinctive role? Yeah, I do. It's called a field of practice and a field of knowledge. And it's why it takes two years in a graduate program to actually come into contact with all that knowledge, because, like medicine, design has developed specialties. I think that for especially more complex problems, there are strategies that you can't learn on a weekend or a week. And I think that that is what we should be calling design.

You touched on something interesting there in how this word "design" has become so broad. There is a difference between a design strategist and an interface designer and a graphic designer. There's this move to be multidisciplinary or a generalist designer but that's so hard to actually do. How do

we think about organizing design, about being multidisciplinary and generative and not territorial? What is the balance between being a part of the team? Having these different roles, while also not entrenching different fields of study?

KE Historically, design has been taught and organized around output: you had interiors, you had communication, you had product. I think the modern era is better served by stepping away from output as being the focal point of the training.

I think that a designer who wants to work in the fields like Maura and myself, in food sustainability and healthcare, you have to assume you are one of many people at a table, and you need to be curious about those adjacent fields. If you're a designer working in healthcare, you probably want to understand what epidemiologists do. You probably want to understand what statisticians or health service researchers do. You don't need to be a leading expert in health economics, but you need to know when to turn to them and you need to know what they are, what their role is likely to be. Looking at different specialties and being adjacent-aware is something that has to be taught. I don't think it's necessarily native for designers.

MS What is it that you're looking for as a designer? What's not only the curiosity you bring, but the lens through which you're observing the world? What's your way of learning and thinking about a given environment or context?

For me, I'm always looking for what the incentives are that are activating or catalyzing a system. Where are the barriers, whether they're intentional or not? How can players or actors in a system find purpose, and how does that context of interaction play out?

That's not an output. I think that's why asset-based community development is so interesting to me, because I'm looking at the pieces and interactions of the contexts. Kim and I both were students of

Chuck Owen, who was all about the structures and elements and functions of systems, so we were educated to look at the world that way. I think the legacy of ID is in thinking about our world in those detailed parts and then recognizing how intentionally or unintentionally those were all designed.

Weslynne Ashton is a professor at the Illinois Institute of Technology with a joint appointment at the Stuart School of Business and ID. She also co-directs ID's Food Systems Action Lab.

John Payne is the head of design at Public Policy Lab and was an associate professor at ID, where he focused on design for technology and society from 2020 to 2023.

How can design make the biggest impact?

–with Weslynne Ashton & John Payne

Over the last decade, there's been an increasing awareness that design cannot and should not be employed solely to maximize profit. The tools of the designer can improve the world, whether that means creating a more equitable society or increasing environmental considerations. Design for social good is a growing area of design practice, but this shift also does not mean we leave corporate clients behind.

What is the role of more traditional design practices within a socially conscious design field?

Weslynne, I'd like to start with a question for you. Your background is not in design. You come from an environmental engineering/environmental science background. I'm wondering if you could talk about where design came into your work and how your background influences your perspective on design and the role of design?

WA   I started my career as an environmental engineer but I would say that I've been practicing design without knowing that it was design for a long time.

In my final semester of undergraduate, I took a course that was called The Politics of Sustainable Development, and I was introduced to the concept of industrial ecology, which is how we design our industrial systems so that they might be more ecological and operate in harmony with nature. I loved this concept because up until that point, the work that I had been doing was all about understanding environmental impacts of various activities, like how to clean up a lot of the pollution that we had created. Then here's this concept that says, "All right, let's not just clean up the pollution, but let's think about how can we design out the pollution from the get-go."

For graduate school, I chose a program in industrial ecology with this design mindset without having any of the design tools. I really didn't formally get introduced to design until several years into my position at Illinois Tech. We have this interprofessional projects program at the undergraduate level that all of our undergraduates have to take, and about two years into being an assistant professor here, I was invited to participate in what was called the IPRO 2.0, which was trying to bring in more design tools into the IPRO led by Jeremy Alexis along with five or six faculty from across the institution who were trained in design thinking as a part of this IPRO redevelopment process.

That was my first foray into formal design tools, and I take little snippets here and there and try to inject them into my classes. I officially joined ID in the fall of 2020 after some more in-depth interaction with faculty and students.

John, you're the director of service design at Verizon, and you're also the chair of the Public Policy Lab, where you've done a lot of work around designing for healthcare. How does that relate to work at Verizon and vice versa? How do you see these things fitting together?

JP Service design is the thread between the two roles that I currently hold as chair of the board at Public Policy Lab and as head of service design at Verizon. Service design is a practice that allows a group of people to engage with the design artifacts, the events around those artifacts, and the outcomes in peer-based ways when facilitated as a practice.

The Public Policy Lab is a nonprofit service design consultancy that works exclusively with government agencies, philanthropies, and research institutions to develop human-centered strategies for social innovation. In particular, they focus on developing policies and services through the research, designing, and testing phases. Bringing service design into that realm is a fairly new construct. It's not the typical way that government agencies do this work.

At Verizon, service design is also a fairly new discipline. It's housed within a much larger design organization that is much more well-established but over the past four years or so, we've introduced service design approaches to address the deeply complex problems that telecom faces when interacting with their customer base, which for Verizon, is about a third of the country. So there's a significant amount of complexity in interacting with that broad set of people.

None of our favorite interactions are customer service interactions with a telecom company so it's actually a really wonderful laboratory for bringing service practices into the organization because there's so much coordination that is required.

It would be really easy to see those as two very different goals, very different activities. When I talk with younger people interested in design, they are frustrated with the big corporations that are governing so much of our lives and the profit motive that we see. I'm not asking you to speak for Verizon, but comparing a for-profit company versus a nonprofit, does service design mean different things? Do the goals of for-profit and nonprofit organizations overlap at all?

JP While the process is the same, it's actually having very different impacts on the two simply because of the way the organizations are structured. Verizon's essentially a laboratory for how to do this at a significant scale while the Public Policy Lab is a small nonprofit consultancy doubling down on the true nature of human-centered service design, in that it's about bringing the public into the process and allowing them a voice through policy creation and public service creation processes where they didn't have a voice in the past. It's about representing the needs and desires and lives of the public – in particular, at risk and underrepresented communities – in the design process.

At Verizon, it has useful effects on the consumer experience, so that's the baseline. But the effect it's having within the organization is a unifying effect where the different groups from our technology organization, from our product management organization, from a marketing organization, as well as our customer experience organization, which I'm a part of, all have roles to play in how an experience of a consumer unfolds. The choreography lends itself to allowing teams to see where their roles manifest, how those touchpoints reach out to the customer, and how those interactions with a customer all need to coordinate with each other. Simply the practice of the work helps to unify the approach of the organization in producing services.

70

Weslynne, you said that you were doing design before you realized it was design. Can you talk more about that? How do you see the role of the designer in these big complex problems?

WA I come from a systems-design perspective: How do we understand the current systems that we're operating in? What are their goals? Who are the key stakeholders? What are their interactions? What are the feedback mechanisms? What are the opportunities for change? I think designers have an important role to help show the system, these relationships, and really visualize that in a way that people can see and relate with.

It's also about visioning and thinking about how we can create new visions of the future through prototyping, looking at changes that can be made at various scales, making those changes, learning from them, and adapting. Designers also have an important role in facilitating, convening, and bringing different groups of people together to help bring out a better understanding of systems, creating plural visions of the future, and pathways to help get there.

One of the courses that I teach right now at ID is around design for a change in climate. What are the fundamental things that designers need to know about climate change? Then can the set of skills and the designer's way of working be applied to climate change, either within a private company or with a government agency or a broader system? So we're playing around with different types of tools to help build design capacity for climate change, as well as applying design tools to address climate challenges.

I'm wondering if these processes, these ways of working, need to be done by designers? Are you teaching primarily people who will be self-identifying as designers, or do these tools and methodologies have a context where there might be no designer presence?

WA   I have a multilevel answer to that. I sit in a joint appointment between design and the Stuart School of Business. I'm teaching business school students on one hand and design students on the other. On the ID side, I try to expose designers to broader systems thinking, environmental, and social issues. Basically, how do we measure the impacts, and then how do we develop design tools to mitigate those impacts? On the business side, it is also exposing them to sustainability issues, but also design thinking and the role of design in there.

Then through various projects that I have been working on, mostly in Chicago, there has been a concerted effort to bridge design practice and share those design skills with our partners, through a co-design approach: recognizing that we can build design capacity, mindsets, skills, and particular tools with partners.

> **I see people talking a lot about wanting to make everyone a designer and make these design tools available. There's a push to be multidisciplinary or interdisciplinary until you get into the project itself and things become very territorial. How do you think about the organization of teams and the role of design in these complex problems?**

JP   In Kevin Slavin's article "Design as Participation," he writes: "Designers of complex adaptive systems are not strictly designing systems themselves. They are hinting those systems toward anticipated outcomes from an array of interrelated systems."* I start with that quote because that's a framing mechanism that I use in both spheres. In Public Policy Lab, any introduction of a new public service or a revision to a public service exists in a very complex existing ecosystem and our ability as designers. We are participants in a complex system, and we're able to change parts of it, introduce new stimuli, and hopefully move things forward. Then

Kevin Slavin, "Design as Participation," *Journal of Design and Science*, February 26, 2016. https://doi.org/10.21428/a39a747c

at Verizon, there's a lot of it on the inside of the organization in how we reveal to the consumer the coordination of our experiences. I'd say the role of the designer in both instances has a strong facilitation component. The mindset of the designer is one where we are going to get together and create something as opposed to deciding on something.

WA I think that mindsets are really important. It speaks to how we are training designers to show up. Are we training them to show up as the experts with particular skills or as participants and facilitators on equal footing? I think the recognition that everyone can create and has that potential is so important, but we don't necessarily have the skills and opportunity to do it. Particularly, when we think about under-resourced communities, both in the US and abroad, there's a dearth of opportunities for people to exercise that creativity, which is not to say that it doesn't happen. There are breakthrough cases of people who, despite whatever their circumstances, are able to come up with new inventions and escape from wherever they are with innovations, but maybe we need to start that training for creativity a lot earlier in life. Do we need to be teaching design thinking in elementary schools?

It's a cliché at this point to say that design is problem-solving. Yes, design is problem-solving, but that's actually just a very small part of it. It's sort of the hammer and nail situation where if you keep telling yourself that design is problem-solving then everything can be solved with design. What I love about what both of you are saying is that the solution is much more complex — if there even is a solution — it's much more interdisciplinary. Design's role is not actually in the solving but in the invention; it is in the platform creation. This idea of design as platform creator or design as, I don't know, cultural inventor seems much more generative and generous than design as hero.

JP I couldn't agree more. I've been a designer long enough to have been at the beginnings of

73

the introduction of human-centered design as a practice, and now it is really the primary expression of design and problem-solving that is at the center of that. That enabled the practice of design to be more widely adopted – which is wonderful – but to your point, it's also quite limiting. We are not caring for the other side of it that you described as design as cultural invention. There are many disciplines that solve problems. There are many fewer disciplines that create cultural artifacts, processes, services, events. Design isn't the only one that does that, but that side of our practice needs to be recognized and talked about and brought to the fore.

> **What are the skills or the ideas or the methods that we could be teaching designers to be thinking more expansively when they are injecting themselves or being asked to be a part of these larger multidisciplinary teams?**

WA The entry point for most designers, working either in the public or private sector, is that you are issued a problem to solve. Often, there's a scope of work, a brief that sets the parameters of the understanding of what the challenge is. There's a certain number of hours that you're expected to spend working on that project. But it takes much more than that to really be able to understand the systemic challenge. So in a way, a designer has to make the case for why the organization should take a more systems-based approach and try to tackle something that's bigger than what they got in the design brief. We talk about using design to better understand the problem and reframe the problem for your clients or whomever you're working with, but I think it's also important to understand the intervention points and the opportunities for leverage. There are times when all you might be able to do is try to reduce the service time or the amount of time spent on dealing with a particular problem, and there may be other opportunities where you can also show opporunties for making a larger change.

say, climate change. To me, it seems like a logical progression, and it's an exciting one – just the way I felt early on when I discovered and started to practice design in the business space.

WA Anijo Mathew, the dean of ID, talks about this eighty-five-year history in eras. In each era, we don't leave things behind, but we're building upon. We expect to continue to work with industry and to use human-centered design tools, but we're in a yet unnamed era of design that is more civic engaged, that is thinking about how we tackle these bigger problems.

On many levels, people are looking for more purpose. Organizations are also grappling with their purpose and how to live up to that purpose. It's not just about being the most profitable. How do you be profitable while serving a bigger purpose? Purpose, I think, needs to be the North Star. What are we working toward? There are going to be roles that business will maintain and roles for the public sector, and there are going to be collaborations across the two.

We're going to see more and more people going throughout their careers between the public and private sectors, and that line is really blurred. There's definitely still space and opportunities for our work to be valuable to industry – most of our students are going to look for jobs in the private sector – but more and more, there are opportunities in the public sector for them to connect, too.

Anijo Mathew is dean and a professor at ID, and the director of the ID Academy. His research focuses on entrepeneurship and urban technology.

Where must design go next?

–with Anijo Mathew

If design is a form of cultural invention, then the history and future of design are deeply connected to larger cultural and societal forces. As we look to the future of design, ID Dean Anijo Mathew identifies three forces that will force design to evolve yet again: distributed trust networks, artificial intelligence (AI), and conscious actioning. Design – in all its forms – must grapple with these issues and work with others across a range of disciplines to imagine futures.

How, then, do you design design? What is the future of design practice? How do you set up academic institutions to thrive under rapid change? What can we learn from design history to point toward a better future?

You were recently appointed dean of the Institute of Design. Can you tell me a little bit about how you see your role and what you want to do as dean?

AM Being the dean of the Institute of Design is both a privilege and an honor, but it's also a little bit scary because you're standing on the shoulders of giants who came before me. Former directors have had films made about them and books written about them, so it's a little intimidating but it's super exciting for me because I feel that one of the big things that I inherited is the transitions over time that the Institute of Design has gone through. One way to think about these transitions is to think about the transitions that the design field has had over the last few years, and ID is symbolic or emblematic of those transitions. I am in the fourth era of the Institute of Design and I like to call it an "era in process," because I'm not a hundred percent sure what to call it yet. In order to understand this era, we need to understand the three preceding eras that came before it.

The first era was that of experimentation. As you may know, the Institute of Design was founded as The New Bauhaus and was the direct descendant of the Bauhaus in Germany by the Hungarian immigrant László Moholy-Nagy. His driving factor for the Institute of Design, or The New Bauhaus at that time, was that the Industrial Revolution was making it incredibly cheap and accessible. Products were becoming accessible to a lot of people, yet the production had this robotic, mundane aspect to it. What he wanted The New Bauhaus to do was to bring a little bit of craft, a little bit of design, into that production value. This was the birth of modernism. So a lot of the ideas came from Europe, from Switzerland, from Germany, and that translated into an era of experimentation at ID.

In the 1950s, a new director, Jay Doblin, came in. Doblin brought in the idea that it is not just enough to be experimenting or prototyping, you also need to think about products and services from a systems level. This is the second era, where ID pioneered the concept of systems design. Doblin and the faculty members at that time were really good at creating these large system solutions to the problems of our time.

Then in the 1990s, another significant change happened at ID, and this was the pioneering of the human-centered design era, or as we know it now, design thinking. Patrick Whitney and several faculty members here at ID said that it's not enough to look at systems; we have to understand the users and the human beings that are in the system using these things. That expanded thinking allowed organizations to shift from, at that time, shareholder points of view to human points of view. This change was significant because you could make products or services that were making a profit for the company, but not really addressing the needs of the user. For many schools, as you know, this is the era that we are in.

What I am now leading is what we call the fourth era of ID. This is an era where it's not just about the complexities of the systems, or the velocities required for production, but how to bring those two things together. Say you are designing for public health or you're designing new food systems, or you are employing generative AI, this is a completely different type of design. It's designed around complexity and understanding a large number of stakeholders. Value exchanges are not easy. There are no easy transactions of value, and you have to map all of that.

If I were to take a shot at defining this era, it is that we are now dealing with multigenerational change. We are dealing with things that will not just affect one generation, but multiple generations in the future. If you designed a bottle – let's say a smart water bottle – the impact of that design is probably going to be felt by one generation of users. But if you design a health system for India, the impact of that is going to be felt by multiple generations of users. This is where design is playing a role, and this is where ID is moving. I feel this is what all design should be focused on in the future.

A couple years ago you wrote a piece for _Medium_ called "'Design+' The New Normal,"*, which, to me, is perhaps a way to start to articulate this new phase. Can you tell me what you mean by Design+?

AM I think this new era of design, which I like to call Design+, is going to pull from human-centered design, which uses principles of systems design, which uses concepts of experimentation within it. The way it's going to translate into our everyday life is that these problems that we are facing are too complex to be solved by designers alone. One of the big changes that design education needs to go through is a release of the hubris that we can actually do it all. If you think about the standard design studio, it's about an individual student learning how to become a designer. When I went through architecture school, the only thing that I heard was, "Oh, you know these great architects that came before you? One day you're going to become one of those. And your goal through the studio is to figure out how to get to that point."

The truth is most of us are never going to become a Rem Koolhaas or a Yves Béhar or a Jony Ive, but we will have an impact on the world. The way we have impact in the world is by collaborating with other people who look very different from us. Design+ is the idea that design plus an allied field can actually create more value than design doing anything on its own. It is these fields coming together that allow us to solve complex problems. The concept is quite simple, right?

One of the things that both fields have to do, but designers in particular have to do, is release the hubris so that we create new mechanisms to collaborate with these fields. I believe that the next era

* Anijo Mathew, "'Design+': The New Normal," _Medium_, October 23, 2020. https://anijomathew.medium.com/design-the-new-normal-76827b57aaae.

of design is going to be the development of theories, frameworks, tools, methods for this collaborative stance. It is the ability for designers to express to an allied field – let's say computer science or public health or engineering – that this is what we bring to the table and this is what we ask of you. When we do that, you can actually come together in interdisciplinary or transdisciplinary ways to solve complex problems.

> **Something that I really liked in the piece in _Medium_ is that designers should think like APIs. Can you tell me about this metaphor, and why this is so helpful for you for this new era?**

AM   An API is an application programmable interface. The easiest way to explain this is that when you have two software systems that talk to each other, each calls for certain data from the other without actually giving up all the data. The idea is that not all proprietary information is shared, but enough is shared that the other software system can take that information and translate it for its own use.

For example, let's say you have a _New York Times_ map on crime data. What the _New York Times_ is doing is calling Google Maps and saying, "Hey, give me the map for New York or Manhattan and drop in these stories that we have of crime that happened in Manhattan into the map." So Google Maps gives the _New York Times_ the map data, the geolocation data, and the _New York Times_ gives to Google Maps the data that they have in the form of stories and narratives. Together, then, they can come up with this visual representation of crime data in New York.

Now, if you take that same idea and translate it into design, the API model means that designers have to understand what the linkages are when they connect with another allied field. You can't just walk into a room and say, "Let's collaborate." When you do that, in most cases, what happens is that it's a multidisciplinary collaboration. The disciplinary boundaries never really go away, and the people just do what they were taught to do.

One of the things we want to get to is this concept where those disciplinary boundaries slowly disappear, and we try to address the problem as a cohesive unit. In order to do that, you need to understand what the linkages are. You need to know how you can translate your disciplinary knowledge into that nondisciplinary person's vocabulary. You need to have mechanisms by which you can parse that allied field's vocabulary and parse that into design knowledge. You need to express values that eventually become outcomes that are expressed internally and externally. What that means is if you are not gaining anything from this relationship, you're never going to go back to this relationship. You need to have outcomes that are expressed externally so that these two disciplines actually give birth to something bigger than if each of those disciplines try to do it on their own.

> When I hear you talk about the way designers need to think about the way that teams collaborate and about shared outcomes and values, I can't help thinking about this through the lens of somebody who is leading an institution. Can you be a little meta for a second and tell me about how you're actually thinking about this in your role? Is being dean a type of design?

AM One hundred percent. I use the same conceptual frameworks in the structure of my activities every day. Let me give you an example of this. The first thing that I did when I became dean was to reach out to the other deans in the university and say, "Design is a catalyst. It's only when we work together can design actually lead to output. So what are some of the ways that we can work together?" We need to invest in the outward and build collaborations outside of our comfort zones so that we can actually get to the bigger multigenerational problems.

What's really interesting for me is that the world has a better appreciation of what design can bring to the table thanks to things like design thinking, which you may or may not subscribe to. We definitely don't at ID. We think design thinking is a reduction of the complexities of design, but it has enabled non-designers to understand the value of design. A big part of my job is to reach out to these organizations and these companies and say, "How can ID work with you?" This manifests in collaborations that probably wouldn't have existed in previous times. The University of Chicago has established a Design Lab at ID to help with healthcare outcomes at the hospital at University of Chicago. We have companies that are interested in prosthetics design reaching out to ID to help them think about generative design and human-centered approaches to creating these prosthetics. None of this is unique, but in the sense that it leads to this whole concept of complexity and velocity working together to create multigenerational change, that's where it gets super exciting.

What's really interesting to me in everything you've been talking about so far is that technology is not central here. I don't mean that to sound Luddite or that it's not driven by technology, but everything you are talking about is still driven by people, it's driven by collaboration. Often when you hear people talk about the future of design, they're talking about it through the lens of technology: How is artificial intelligence going to change design? How is virtual reality going to change design? Can you talk about the role of technology here, and how that fits into this larger cultural shift in design that you're talking about?

AM To understand all of this, one must contextualize it: without basing it on a technological revolution that we are in, none of this would be possible. The foundation of all of this is the technology that is driving it but the role of the designer is not to romance the technology. That's the role of the engineer or the software scientist. If we start romancing the technology, then there's nobody thinking about how it'll be applied in the real world. This is what I tell my students: it's not our job to romance technology. It is our job to critique the technology in both positive and negative ways so that it can be applied in the context of human activity or humanity-centered activities, whether that be for sustainability, climate change, healthcare, public health, education, whatever it is. It is our job to do that. An engineer may not think about that, but that's not their job to think about that.

I believe that there are three seismic forces that are acting upon design that all designers should be conscious of. The first one is distributed trust. This notion that trust in institutions is eroding is something we should pay attention to. What that means is we already have technologies that question the foundational belief we have in financial institutions. Think of cryptocurrencies or blockchain. We have a group of people that are starting to question how public health can move away from hospitals to community-based care. What all of this is leading to is the emergence of a new type of network that is centered around distributed trust. That trust is not centered around one individual or one institution, but dispersed in the community, whether it be through blockchain, where we can certify that a certain action was done as a community or in the form of health outcomes or food systems that is governed by a group of people rather than an institution.

The second change is artificial intelligence. We saw the birth of some revolutionary ideas just in the last few months with ChatGPT and DALL-E 2 and Midjourney that are going to change the way we think about everything, including design. What are you going to do if DALL-E 2 can create a hundred options in 10 seconds? What is the role of the designer then? Sam Altman, the founder of ChatGPT, says that it is the intersection of humans and technology that's going to lead to the changes that he envisions through ChatGPT. It's the interpretation of that data. It is

It's not our job to romance technology.

It is our job to critique the technology in both positive and negative ways so that it can be applied in the context of human activity.

—Anijo Mathew

the manipulation of that data. It's the use of predictive analytics so we can say, "We have a thousand options, but the only three that work in the context of rural Africa are these three because we know inherently what the human system looks like."

This leads to the third seismic change that's happening: conscious actioning. As a society, we are now holding our leaders to a higher standard of action than ever before in human history. We are asking them to be more judicious about the decisions that they're making in thinking about race, ethnicity, health, climate change. It's no longer about the individual. It is about actions that are more conscious and will affect a larger group of people. Here, too, design is going to get impacted. The whole concept of human-centered revolved around the idea that individually, we are going to take charge of the values that are being transferred over to us and that individually we are going to ask for better values. Conscious actioning means that we are going to think beyond the individual to more community-based experiences, more humanity-based experiences. The notion of what value design brings to that conversation is bigger than human-centered design. It's about co-design or engaging communities in the conversation. It's about changing the value exchanges that come from shareholder value to stakeholder value. It's about corporations understanding that this production of wealth and goods is not of an outcome that is conducive to human development as a species.

I believe that in all three of these changes, design will play a major role in the future. The role of the design school is going to change from helping designers create widgets for apps to helping them be part of the team that writes executive orders at the White House. That's the level of change that we are going to see in the next few years.

What makes ID ID? I'm interested in how you think about ID as a brand, as an institution, as thought leader, but also acknowledging that ID is filled with

89

a bunch of individuals who have their own research agendas, their own interests, their own things that they're bringing into the program, whether that's faculty or students or administrators. What is that overlap between the individual and the institution?

AM I think it's really important to think about these things as an administrator of an entity that is filled with entrepreneurs. If you think of every individual faculty member, we encourage them to be their own entrepreneur. We encourage them to have free thought. I think this is something that we should nurture. Having interacted with education systems around the world, I have noticed one thing: the United States has something precious and that is the idea of academia being free to do what they want to do. This is somewhat unique to the US in the sense that faculty members are able to do what they want to do. It's this notion of academic independence or experimentation.

This has nothing to do with tenure or all of the other procedural conversations that we have in universities now. That's not what I'm talking about. What I'm talking about is this combination of freedom, entrepreneurship, the ability for a faculty member to say that I'm going to use my lab or my classroom as a sandbox to think about things that other people are not able to think about. This capacity creates incredible value because it stretches our points of view beyond what capitalism can do. Capitalism can be a great driving force for change, but it is bound by the idea of economic development or capital development or shareholder value. Education – or academia – has the ability to think beyond that, to question some of the things that a capitalistic enterprise might do, to stretch or force or encourage that enterprise to think beyond what it's doing right now. I think this is the ideal of the ID brand. The ID brand is this ability for us to be ahead of industry.

We are not a training ground for industry. The only way that we can do this is to bring a group of really interesting, crazy people who are willing to take risks and give them the freedom to do what they want to do within boundary conditions of ethics and education and knowledge creation and outcome-oriented structures that all knowledge must be free and open to everybody.

To me, this is how ID differentiates itself from other design schools. We have a group of faculty members who are encouraged to think about these multigenerational problems that other design schools may or may not be thinking about. It creates this platform, this sandbox approach, and tells the faculty members, "Hey, if you want funding for this, I'll find you the funding. That's my job to get you the money to do this radical thing. You don't have to worry about that. If you want to do this without funding, that's fine, too." If a student body comes in and says, as they do at ID, that diversity is an important conversation to have and that diversity should be part of our core curriculum, we talk about that as a faculty. We don't ignore the students and just say, "Hey, here's what we have taught for the last twenty years and nothing's going to change." I think that's the idea of ID that keeps me here. I didn't go to ID. I'm not an ID graduate, but I love ID because of that idea.

I want to underscore this idea that design school is not a training ground for industry, but is actually a playground to change industry. This view speaks to both everything we've talked about: all of these changes in design, they're also correcting blind spots, making adjustments. They're all working toward a better future. That's what design school is for. It's to change the industry.

AM And the interesting thing is that this also leads to incredible career outcomes for our students. Because we are training them to take on leadership roles, they actually get into senior positions in companies. The average increase in salary is about 166 percent if you come to ID. Nearly 3 times [the medium design salary]. We have the highest median income range. The *Wall Street Journal* tracked income range for design schools, and we have by far the highest median income range for any design school in the country. It also speaks to this kind of industry mindset. If you give them people to do the work, they will hire you and they'll make you do work. If you give them people who can question the practices, they will hire you and ask you to question practices. Our job is to create conversation, to question, to critique. To say, "Hey, what if we brought artificial intelligence into supply chain management? What would that look like for our users?" That's a different conversation from, how do you design a website for the user?

Contributors

WESLYNNE ASHTON is a professor at the Illinois Institute of Technology with a joint appointment at the Stuart School of Business and the Institute of Design (ID). She also co-directs ID's Food Systems Action Lab.

KIM ERWIN is an associate professor at ID, where she focuses on healthcare design and design methods. She also directs ID's Equitable Healthcare Action Lab. An expert in healthcare design, she applies design methods to complex systems and develops novel solutions to address healthcare's frontline problems. Specifically, Erwin applies human-centered design and communication methods to build teams, identify opportunities, and tailor interventions to real-world settings, to accelerate adoption by patients and clinical staff.

TOMOKO ICHIKAWA is an associate teaching professor at ID, where she focuses on visual communication. She believes that good design requires analysis and should be driven by content and context, and she applies that philosophy as an educator and practitioner of clear, effective visual communication design of complex information.

ANIJO MATHEW is dean and a professor at ID, and the director of the ID Academy. His research focuses on entrepreneurship and urban technology, and he evaluates new models of innovation enabled by technology and media convergence through the lenses of design fiction, design-led innovation, and entrepreneurship. He works with global organizations to adapt and change strategic responses to transforming technologies.

MATT MAYFIELD is associate dean of academics and administration at ID and director of the Master of Design and Master of Design Methods graduate programs. His applied research extends across the domains of design, consumer behavior, product and service strategy, and computing technology for Fortune 500 companies.

JOHN PAYNE is the head of design at Public Policy Lab and was an associate professor at ID from 2020 to 2023, where he focused on design for technology and society. He taught digital service design as well as an emerging tech survey introducing students to a number of emerging technologies and investigating their societal implications. He has been a thought leader in the human-centered interaction design community since the early 2000s.

ZACH PINO is an assistant professor of data-driven design at ID, where he designs with generative algorithms, machine learning models, wearable technologies, and reactive materiality. He aims to create data visualizations, personalized objects, accessible interactive experiences, and fabrication processes that educate, include, surprise, recollect, and encourage contemplation. He holds a bachelor

of arts degree from the University of Chicago and a master's degree in design from the School of the Art Institute of Chicago.

RUTH SCHMIDT is an associate professor at ID, where she focuses on behavioral design. Her teaching and research concentrate on the intersection of the deep understanding of contextualized and latent user needs achieved through humanity-centered design with the "evergreen" insights into human judgment, decision-making, and behavior gleaned through behavioral economics.

MAURA SHEA is an associate professor at ID, where she focuses on evolving community-led development methods and approaches. She is also the co-director of the ID Food Systems Action Lab. Working for over a decade as an innovation leader in national nonprofit networks, Shea is interested in civic and social collaboration and how human-centered design can support equity and inclusion through the experiences of belonging and community well-being.

CARLOS TEIXEIRA is the Charles L. Owen Professor of Systems Design Design at ID, where he teaches graduate courses and advises doctoral students on the strategic use of design capabilities in complex spaces of innovation. He is also director of the Action Labs and has his own ID Action Lab focused on sustainable solutions.

MARTIN THALER is an associate professor at ID, where he focuses on product and environment design. He has taught product design and environmental design at ID full time since 2008. Keenly interested in the fundamentals of design, he provides students with real-world opportunities in hospitals, schools, businesses, and other institutions from which they can experience how design can make a difference in people's lives.

JARRETT FULLER is a designer, writer,

educator, editor, and podcaster. He is an assistant professor of graphic design at North Carolina State University; director of twenty-six, a multidisciplinary design and editorial studio; and host of the design podcast *Scratching the Surface*.

Acknowledgments

Thank you to everyone at ID for their support, collaboration, and partnership throughout this project. It was an honor to be the 2022–23 Latham Fellow.

Special thanks to Kristin Gecan, for her guidance and organization, and to Dean Anijo Mathew for his encouragement and conversations.

Thanks to Jake Anderson at Oro Editions and Curtiss Haug at Graphic Arts Studio.

—JF

Colophon

Published on the occasion of the Institute of Design's eighty-fifth anniversary as part of the 2022-2023 Latham Fellowship.

The conversations included in this publication were originally recorded for season two of the *With Intent* podcast. You can listen to the full conversations at id.iit.edu/podcast.

—Editor/Designer
Jarrett Fuller

—Managing Editor
Jake Anderson

—Copy Editor
Amy Teschner

—Printer
Graphic Arts Studio
Barrington, IL

—Distributor
Oro Editions

—Typefaces
Panama
Sohne

First edition